Johanna Basford

30 Days
of
Creativity

Draw, Colour &
Discover Your Creative Self

EBURY
PRESS

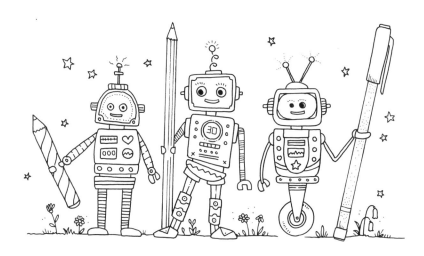

1

Ebury Press an imprint of Ebury Publishing,
20 Vauxhall Bridge Road, London SW1V 2SA

Ebury Press is part of the Penguin Random House group of companies
whose addresses can be found at global.penguinrandomhouse.com

 Penguin
Random House
UK

Copyright © Johanna Basford 2021

Johanna Basford has asserted her right to be identified as the author
of this Work in accordance with the Copyright,
Designs and Patents Act 1988

First published by Ebury Press in 2021
www.penguin.co.uk

A CIP catalogue record for this book is available from the British Library

ISBN 978 1 52914 829 9

 MIX
Paper from
responsible sources
FSC® C018179

Penguin Random House is committed to a
sustainable future for our business, our readers
and our planet. This book is made from Forest
Stewardship Council® certified paper.

Interior designed by Johanna Basford and Sabrina Bowers
Printed and bound in China by Toppan Leefung

Set in Libre Baskerville

This book belongs to

. . . .

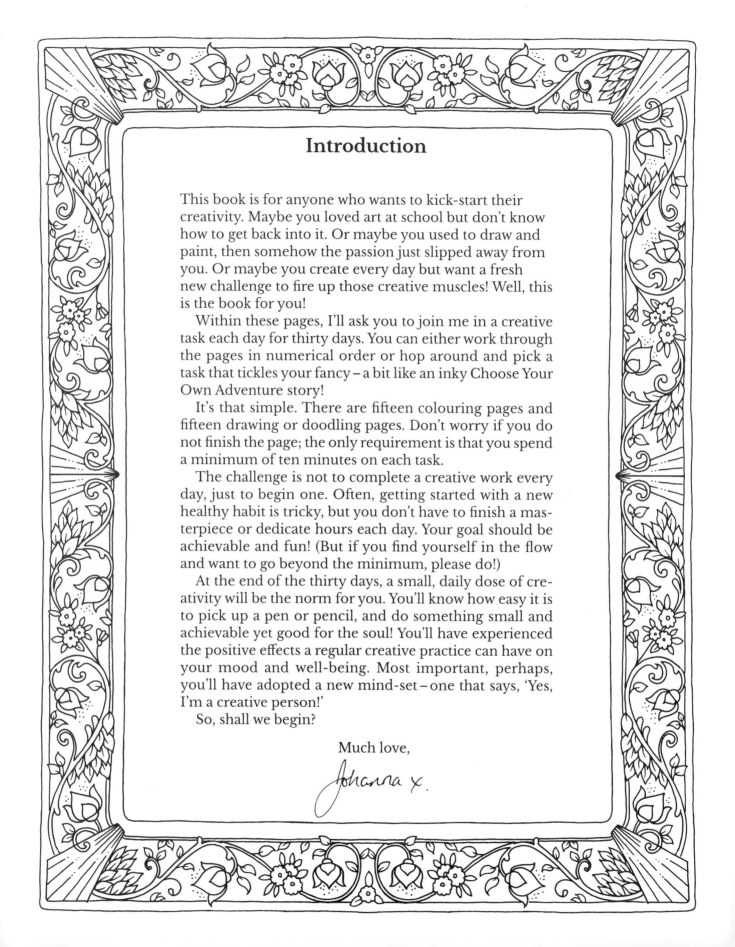

Introduction

This book is for anyone who wants to kick-start their creativity. Maybe you loved art at school but don't know how to get back into it. Or maybe you used to draw and paint, then somehow the passion just slipped away from you. Or maybe you create every day but want a fresh new challenge to fire up those creative muscles! Well, this is the book for you!

Within these pages, I'll ask you to join me in a creative task each day for thirty days. You can either work through the pages in numerical order or hop around and pick a task that tickles your fancy – a bit like an inky Choose Your Own Adventure story!

It's that simple. There are fifteen colouring pages and fifteen drawing or doodling pages. Don't worry if you do not finish the page; the only requirement is that you spend a minimum of ten minutes on each task.

The challenge is not to complete a creative work every day, just to begin one. Often, getting started with a new healthy habit is tricky, but you don't have to finish a masterpiece or dedicate hours each day. Your goal should be achievable and fun! (But if you find yourself in the flow and want to go beyond the minimum, please do!)

At the end of the thirty days, a small, daily dose of creativity will be the norm for you. You'll know how easy it is to pick up a pen or pencil, and do something small and achievable yet good for the soul! You'll have experienced the positive effects a regular creative practice can have on your mood and well-being. Most important, perhaps, you'll have adopted a new mind-set – one that says, 'Yes, I'm a creative person!'

So, shall we begin?

Much love,

Johanna x.

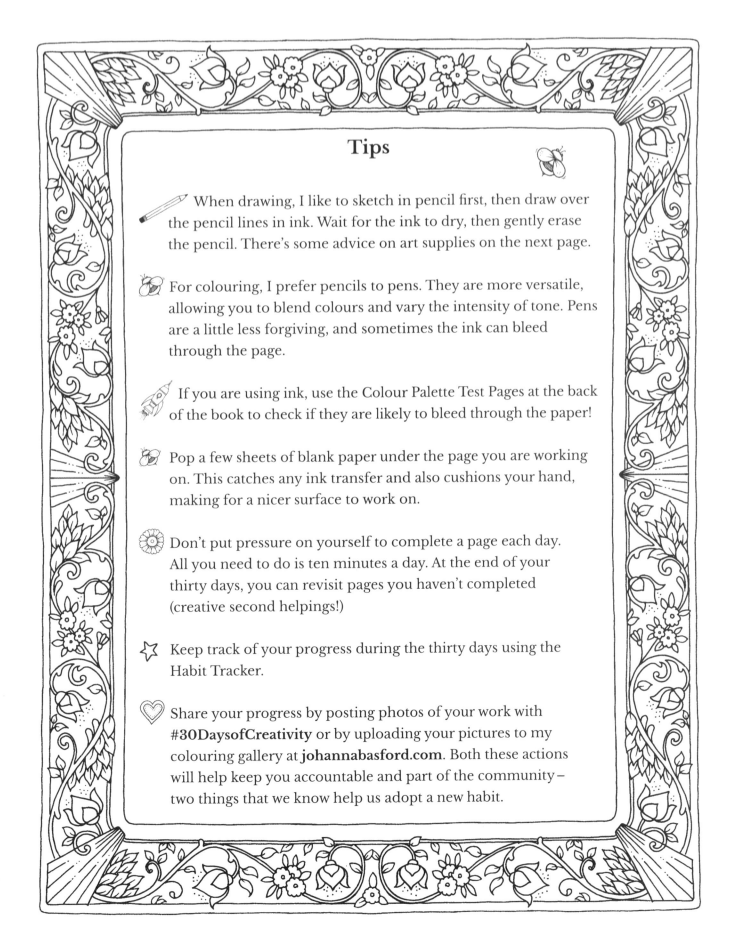

Tips

When drawing, I like to sketch in pencil first, then draw over the pencil lines in ink. Wait for the ink to dry, then gently erase the pencil. There's some advice on art supplies on the next page.

For colouring, I prefer pencils to pens. They are more versatile, allowing you to blend colours and vary the intensity of tone. Pens are a little less forgiving, and sometimes the ink can bleed through the page.

If you are using ink, use the Colour Palette Test Pages at the back of the book to check if they are likely to bleed through the paper!

Pop a few sheets of blank paper under the page you are working on. This catches any ink transfer and also cushions your hand, making for a nicer surface to work on.

Don't put pressure on yourself to complete a page each day. All you need to do is ten minutes a day. At the end of your thirty days, you can revisit pages you haven't completed (creative second helpings!)

Keep track of your progress during the thirty days using the Habit Tracker.

Share your progress by posting photos of your work with **#30DaysofCreativity** or by uploading your pictures to my colouring gallery at **johannabasford.com**. Both these actions will help keep you accountable and part of the community – two things that we know help us adopt a new habit.

Art Supplies

Pencils

I like to sketch things in pencil first using a Staedtler Mars Rotary pencil (a clicky one!), but any pencil will do. Don't go for anything too soft – a B or HB is perfect.

Pens

When it comes to inking artwork, I like a fibre-tipped black ink pen. The fineliner is perfect for this. My favourites are Staedtler Pigment Liners in 0.2 mm size.

Erasers

You will need a clean, white plastic eraser; these lift graphite off beautifully without smudging or ripping the paper. Feeling fancy? I love my battery-powered Derwent eraser – it's great for tiny, precise erasing and also for creating highlights in coloured pencil.

Sharpener

Bigger and more expensive isn't always better. Find a nice sharp one that has a pot for catching the shavings – much less messy! If you need to sharpen a lot of pencils, I recommend a manual rotary sharpener that clamps to your desk instead of an electric one.

Colouring Pencils

You don't need six hundred colouring pencils that cost an arm and a leg! There are plenty of great, affordable sets that give you a lot of colour options without breaking the bank. You'll want a set that is soft enough to blend but hard enough that you can sharpen to a nice point for those small details. I particularly like Staedtler Ergosoft pencils, along with sets by Arteza, Castle Arts, and Faber-Castell.

Other bits and bobs that aren't essential but nice to have:

Compass, protractor, ruler, squared paper, tracing paper, extra drawing paper, gel pens, blender pen, or pencil.

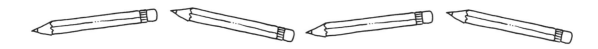

Habit Tracker

Stay accountable on the thirty-day challenge!
Each day that you complete the required ten minutes on a page,
colour a circle. As you start to see those circles fill with colour,
you'll be motivated to keep going and not break the chain!

1	2	3	4	5
6	7	8	9	10
11	12	13	14	15
16	17	18	19	20
21	22	23	24	25
26	27	28	29	30

Taking the thirty-day challenge again?
Get a free download of this Habit Tracker at
johannabasford.com/30days.

I love a cup of tea! Properly brewed, in a teapot and served in a pretty teacup.

Add decorations to the teacups and coffee mugs on the opposite page. Use the designs on this page for ideas and inspiration.

Now we need some cake to go with our tea and coffee . . .

Imagine a lazy Sunday morning, spent visiting quaint little cafés and bakeries.
Sounds heavenly, doesn't it? Whether you enjoy your morning coffee with
a slice of cherry pie or toast smothered in honey,
there's something for everyone in this collage of treats!

Settle down with your pencils and begin colouring your favourite item
on the opposite page!

Enjoying the coffee shop vibes?
Stay a little longer and fill the space on this page
with a few more of your favourite treats.

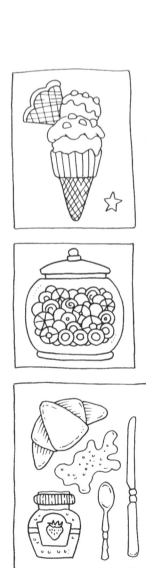
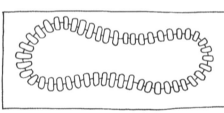

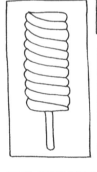

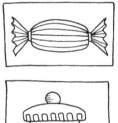

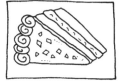

There is something so soothing about working on a symmetrical motif. Complete the nature-themed design on the opposite page, replicating the pattern in the remaining three-quarters. Work in pencil first, then go over the lines in ink and add colour.

Tip: Work from the centre outward and complete each ring of the design before moving on to the next.

In the mood to colour? Grab your pencils and splash a little life onto this page!

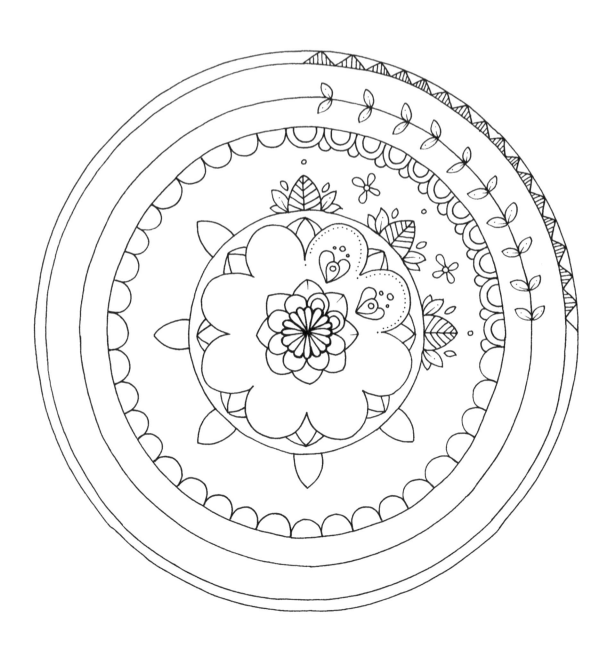

On the opposite page you will find twenty-five imagined blooms, all awaiting your colours.

Don't worry about trying to identify each stem or about colouring them realistically – instead, embrace the mixed-up world of my inky hybrids!

Use the space below to invent a few of your own flowers.

Bringing a few blossoms indoors is a simple way to spread a little cheer.

Drawing flowers has the same effect on me!

Fill these vases with lots of different imagined flowers. Don't get bogged down trying to replicate an exact bloom; just have fun and make them up! Don't forget to add a few leaves and sprigs of foliage too!

PROGRESS, NOT PERFECTION

Marie Forleo often speaks about 'Progress not Perfection' and
it's a concept I wholeheartedly embrace.

Contrary to popular belief, practise does not make perfect. It makes for progress.
We need to let go of this idea of perfection. Perfect is a moving target. We can't all
agree on what exactly it is, so how can we possibly achieve it?

Instead, aim for progress. Progress is definable. Measurable. You can see it!

It's called a 'creative practice' because every day we practise and get a little better.
The sole aim of my work is always to make the next piece of art better than the one
I made before it. Gradual progress. And that should be your aim too!
Practise a little every day and you'll soon see improvement.

Remember when you first went to school and were learning to write? I bet the letters
were a bit wobbly and it was tricky holding that pencil. Well, look at you now!
You can jot down a shopping list with the blink of an eye! Yes, it was hard at the start,
but you kept practising and you got better, and now it's second nature.

Aim for progress. Forget perfection. It doesn't exist anyway.

Progress

not

Perfection

No matter how old we are, a trip to the candy store is
always a treat. Jars of rainbow-coloured sweets, paper bags
stuffed with lemon drops and bonbons, or melty ice lollies –
get your sugar high on paper, without the toothache!

Will you use rainbow colours to add pops of vibrant colour
to these little illustrations? Or will you go for muted
pastel shades and pale candy tones?

Tip: Why not try adding some glitter gel pen details?
Remember to test your pens at the back of the book
to ensure your ink won't bleed through
to the page below!

An inky botanical sphere is the perfect place for special words. Create your own flowery circle on the opposite page, then add a quote or phrase that inspires or creates joy for you.

Tip: I like to draw some of my flowers overlapping the circle and some cropped to the outline. This creates a lovely organic feeling and keeps the entire illustration looking loose and alive!

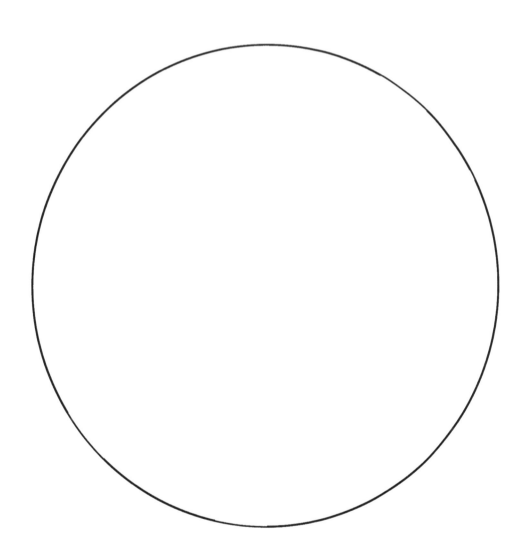

Do you have a passion for pencils? A weakness for washi tape? Me too! Does your heart skip a beat when you see a tin of colouring pencils arranged in neat rainbow order? Mine too!

Art materials are our tickets to adventure. They allow us to draw, colour, and craft – they literally create cheer!

Create your dream set of colouring pencils below or add a splash of colour to the motifs on the opposite page.

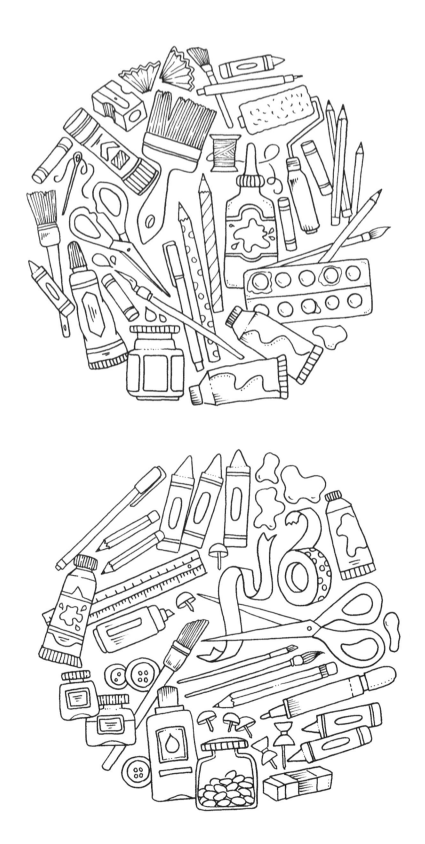

Up, up, and away!

We all need a good adventure from time to time, even if it is just of the daydream variety!

Doodle some patterns on the hot-air balloons opposite and, for a few minutes, allow yourself to drift away into a cloud-filled sky!

Tip: For precise patterns, draw in pencil first, then go over your lines in ink. To create something looser and more free-flowing, just grab your pen and dive in!

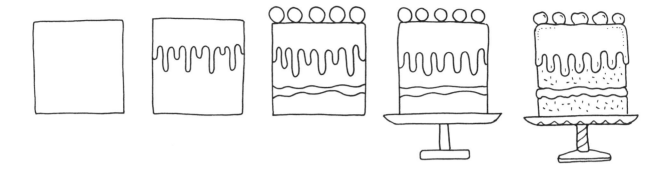

Cake makes everything better. If you want to avoid the washing up, try drawing your cakes instead of baking them! Creating even the fanciest of cakes is easy-peasy.

Grab your pencil and draw a rectangle, then add some drippy icing, a few cherries, and a wobbly line of jam. Add a cake stand. Then grab your pen and ink over your pencil sketch. Ta-da!

Once you have mastered the basic cake method, get fancy! Try triple-layer cakes; add sprinkles and cake toppers, meringues and fruit, flowers and candles. Let your imagination run wild in this inky kitchen!

Use this page to create the cakes of your dreams . . .

DO MORE OF WHAT MAKES YOU HAPPY

Life is short, so we have precious little time to waste on things that don't bring us joy. If you are colouring a page or working on a drawing and it's not going the way you would like, course correct. Make some changes: try a few new colours, add some gel pen details, try adding something new to the composition, listen to some music, or rotate the page and work on it upside down!

Still not feeling it? Turn the page and try something new.

I believe creativity should be *fun*! Challenging, yes, but never tiresome. If it feels like trudging through honey, stop. This is your time.

Some projects and pages are intended to be dipped in and out of; some are never meant to be finished. If you love colouring birds but aren't a fan of architecture, colour more birds, my friend!

Fill your creative practice with things that bring you joy, and have no qualms about saying 'no thank you' to things that feel like a burden.

Do more
of what
makes
you
Happy

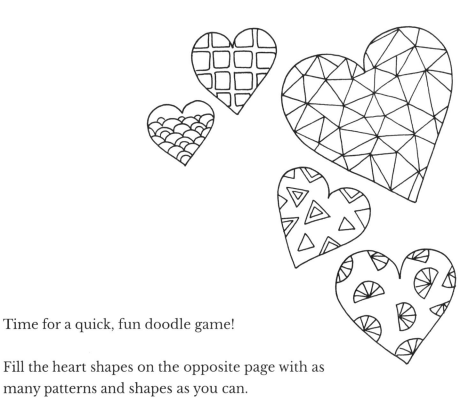

Time for a quick, fun doodle game!

Fill the heart shapes on the opposite page with as many patterns and shapes as you can.

This is a great creative exercise to get you thinking of ways to fill spaces in your pictures. Whether it's a rainbow stripe, a flurry of leaves, or mosaic of tiles, it's useful to have a library of patterns that you can dip into when drawing.

Too many ideas? Keep going! Fill the space on this page with even more hearts, and embellish those too!

Take a dip beneath the ocean waves and explore this inky coral reef. Bring this collection of underwater illustrations alive with ocean-inspired colours and maybe even a little glitter gel pen!

I love small compositions like these on the opposite page – they are perfect for when you don't have much time or just want a small, complete picture in ten minutes or so.

Having fun hanging out beneath the waves? Stay a little longer! Use the space on this page to draw a few tropical fish, a curious sea turtle, or even a sunken treasure chest!

Fill these planters with your own leafy houseplants.

See how many different types of leaves you can draw —
and don't forget to include some cacti and succulents!

Robots! Oh how simple life would be if we just had a few extra hands! As you are colouring these little guys, imagine what super helpful functions they could have in your life. Pencil-Sharpener Robot? Laundry-Folding Droid? Colour a few of your favourites or the entire Robo Squad.

For a shiny metallic effect, experiment with highlights. One way to add some highlights is to use a white or metallic gel pen. Alternatively, you can experiment with 'lifting off' some of the coloured pencil with a white plastic eraser, revealing the paper below. Try a few different methods to see what works best for you.

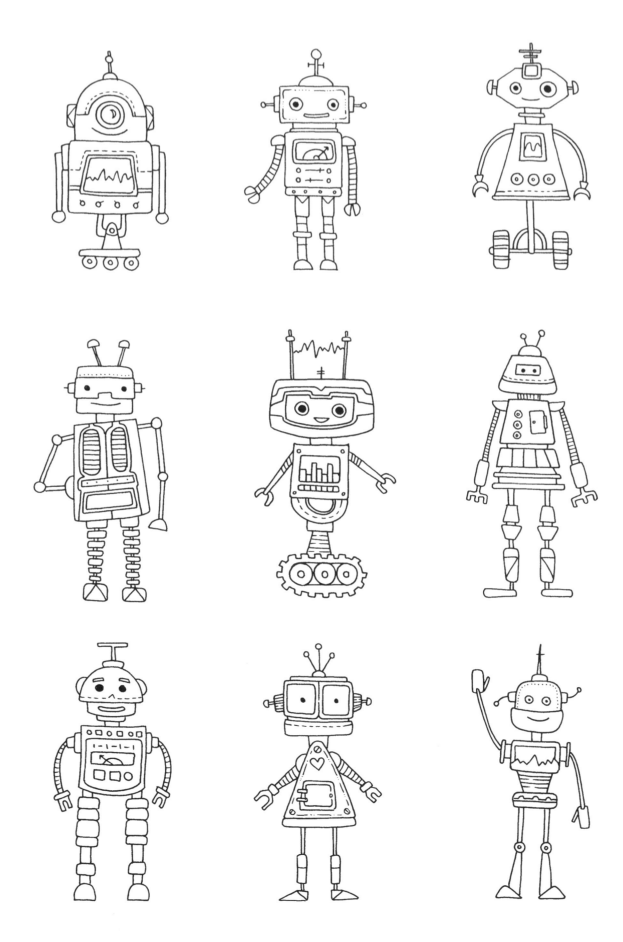

I love a little baking! The simple act of following a recipe and making something delicious and homemade always creates calm in my kitchen.

If you haven't got the time (or the ingredients) to whip up a cake just now, then pick up your pencils and colour these little baking drawings instead!

EVERY CHILD IS AN ARTIST

Have you ever seen a toddler clutching a pack of crayons, wracked with self-doubt? No! They are too busy drawing, letting their creativity spill out of them with wild abandon, and generally living their best lives!

I've always thought these words were Picasso's. Maybe they are, maybe they aren't. Either way, it's a great little reminder that we are all born creative. The need to create and express ourselves is a core part of being human. It's why kids draw on walls and our ancestors painted their caves. So it makes sense that we are drawn to pick up a pencil.

The problem is that we forget. As we get older and find ourselves busy in the act of adulting, we forget to make time for the simple pleasure of creativity. Then we lose our confidence, telling ourselves, 'Oh, I'm not creative. I can't draw' – and before you know it, we are so busy ordering groceries and arranging insurance that we don't have time to draw or colour or paint.

You *are* creative. We all are. We just forget sometimes.

And that's OK, it happens. Life is busy. But when you carve out time for art, something amazing happens. You reawaken that childlike sense of joy, you take a break from the chaos of being a grown-up, and you allow yourself a moment to pause and recharge. You put down your phone.

Here's the good news: you don't need to sign up for an expensive oil painting class or take up sculpture. You are exactly where you need to be. Work through this book, complete the thirty days, and lay the foundations for your creative practice.

Every
child
is an
Artist

Picasso

A recipe passed down the generations or between friends is such a treasure. This is my Gran's Lemon Butter Cake.

Use the opposite page to create an illustrated recipe for one of your favourite cakes.

Lemon Butter Cake

170 g (6 oz.) butter

2 eggs

170 g (6 oz.) caster sugar

170 g (6 oz.) self-raising flour

Juice of 1 lemon

100 g (4 oz.) caster sugar

Blend softened butter and sugar together.

Add eggs and flour.

Spread in a greased and dusted 30 x 20 cm (12" x 8") pan.

Bake 40–45 minutes at 180˚C (350˚F).

Crunchy Topping

Mix lemon juice and sugar to a soft paste and spread on cake while still warm from the oven.

Cut into squares when cold.

Tip: Use the baking illustrations on the previous page
as inspiration for your own delicious doodles!

I adore getting letters in the mail! The sight of a handwritten envelope and a colourful stamp never fail to bring a smile to my face!

Add a little colour to the stamps on the opposite page, and decide from where in the world each began its journey.

This circle is full of little doodles inspired by my life –
the things I love, my hobbies, my work, objects that I see every day.
I call it an 'All about Me' illustration.

Now it's your turn. Fill the outline on the opposite page with
drawings of meaningful items from your life.

Tip: It can help to start by writing a list, noting down everything
that you'd like to include, then begin doodling!

Shake
up a snow globe
and gaze into the mesmerizing
flurry of snowflakes and sparkles! I've always
found these miniature worlds so enchanting.
Use colouring pencils on the next page to bring these little
domes to life.

Want a little more magic? These are the perfect pictures for
some glitter or metallic gel pen detailing!

I often get asked advice on picking colours. If you are feeling a bit unsure,
my top tip is to try a limited colour palette. Select five to six colours from
your pencils – say, three shades of pink, yellow, and a couple of greens –
then colour your picture in *only* those colours! Put the rest of your pencils
away so you aren't tempted to cheat. Reducing the number of
decisions you have to make means picking colours is much
easier, and a limited number of colours ensures
the finished picture will have a
pleasing, coherent
look.

You are never too old for ice cream. Never!

Follow these simple step-by-step guides to create your own glorious selection of ice creams and ice lollies. Draw the first four steps in pencil, then grab your pen and draw over your pencil lines in ink. Wait for the ink to dry before erasing the pencil sketch and adding a dash of colour to make these treats extra tasty!

Once you have mastered the basic method, it's time to get experimental! Add whipped cream, drizzles of sauce, cherries, sprinkles, and as many wafers as you want! The ice cream of dreams knows no boundaries!

Draw your own wondrous ice cream and ice lolly creations here.

INSPIRE, NOT INTIMIDATE

I love sharing pictures of your colouring. When I spot an amazing piece of work, a page completed with such incredible skill that I stop in my tracks to peer closer, I have to share it! These are works of art!

I post these images to inspire – to show what's possible and to prompt us all to try to get better.

It's important, though, to feel inspired when you see those pictures, not intimidated. The person who coloured that page might have been colouring every day for six years. This might be your first attempt! Comparison is the thief of joy. The only work you should compare yours to is the work you created yesterday.

We're each on our own creative journey, and while it's lovely to check in to see the work of others, use it as fuel instead of as a speed bump.

Inspire
not
Intimidate

Sharpen those colouring pencils, and let's bring this freshly picked page to life! Will you go traditional and use nature as your colour palette inspiration? Or will you go bananas (!) and create entirely new varieties of these familiar fruits? Purple pineapples, rainbow raspberries – I can't wait to see what you come up with.

Can you spot a fruit that's often mistaken as a vegetable?

Doodles are inky daydreams. Allow your mind (and your pen!) to wander as you fill the opposite page with loops and squiggles. These loose, carefree drawings are fun to create and can just meander across the page, growing organically.

Create your own inky doodle beginning in the opposite corner and see where your pen takes you!

Bath time! I'm not sure if it's the scent of lavender and sandalwood, the bubbles, or just the tranquil quiet of a candlelit bathroom, but there's something rather blissful about a bath!

Get your bath-time bliss fix by colouring this dainty little bathtub-inspired pattern. I love a busy page like this – it's so easy to tune out and find myself in the flow as I hop from item to item with my colouring pencils. Colour as much or as little as you like. Flood both pages in colour or complete a small section and leave the rest for another day – the choice is yours!

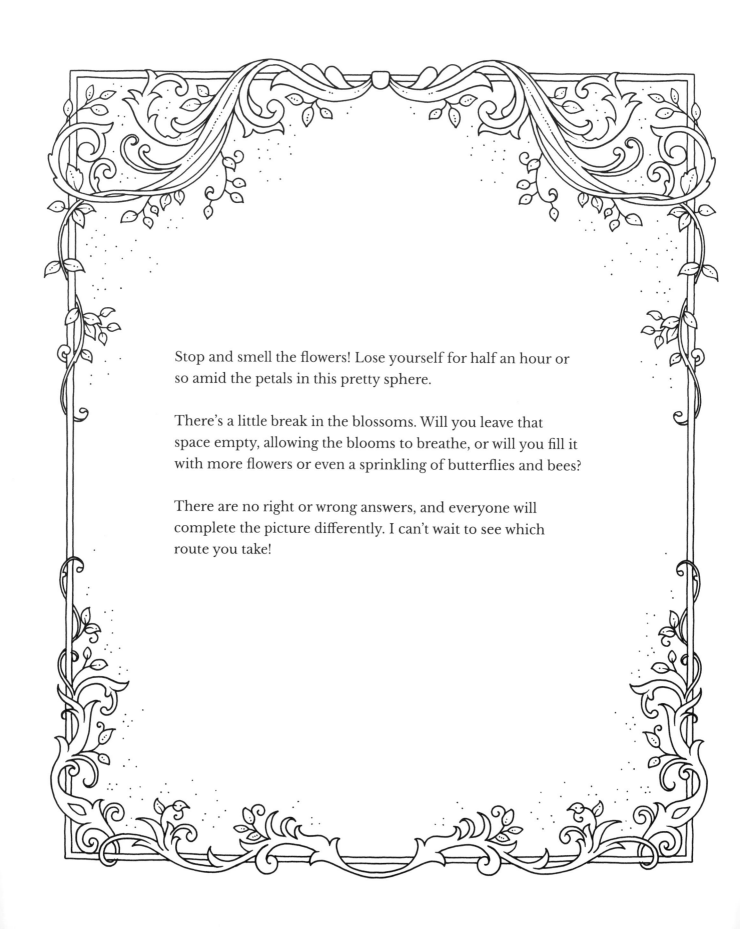

Stop and smell the flowers! Lose yourself for half an hour or so amid the petals in this pretty sphere.

There's a little break in the blossoms. Will you leave that space empty, allowing the blooms to breathe, or will you fill it with more flowers or even a sprinkling of butterflies and bees?

There are no right or wrong answers, and everyone will complete the picture differently. I can't wait to see which route you take!

Let's go fly a kite! Add patterns, shapes, and details to the kites on the opposite page. Stripes, stars, polka dots, zigzags – anything goes! And when your drawings are complete, add a splash of bright colour before your kites fly away into the sky!

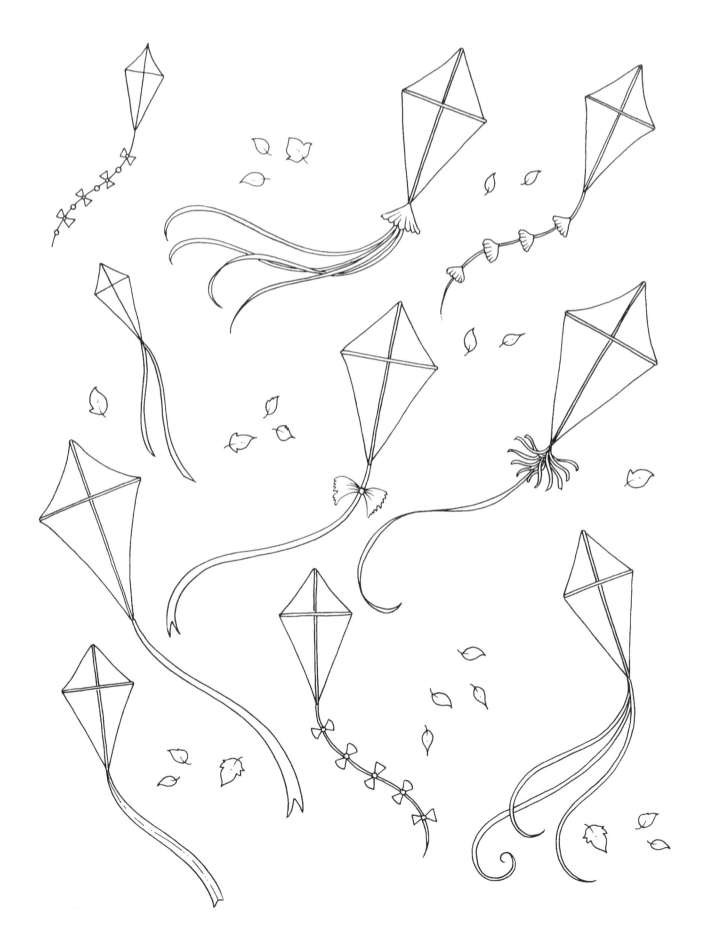

GO OUTSIDE THE LINES

True confession: I go over the lines all the time. If you've ever watched one of my live videos, you'll know this. And you know what? I don't care – and neither should you!

Those lines are just a guide. It's up to you how to complete the picture. You are the artist. The prompts and instructions in this book are simply suggestions. If you feel like doing something different, please do. Creativity is wandering off the page, straying from the path, and experimenting. It's about making it up as you go along. Think of my books as the starting point: where you end up is in your hands (literally!).

There are no rules or one single correct answer here – this isn't a maths class! If you go over the lines when you are colouring, good for you. I love a little freestyling!

There are also no right or wrong colours. This is why I'm not really a fan of painting by numbers or recommending specific colour palettes. I think part of the joy of colouring is selecting your colours, seeing what works and what doesn't. In short, experimenting. We aren't aiming to re-create the same finished picture over and over again; that would be 'manufacturing' and we're in the business of 'creating.' I love that I never see the same picture twice. The unique way you approach a page is what makes this pursuit fun.

So the next time you go over the lines, smile. It's just your inner artist escaping!

Go
outside
the
lines

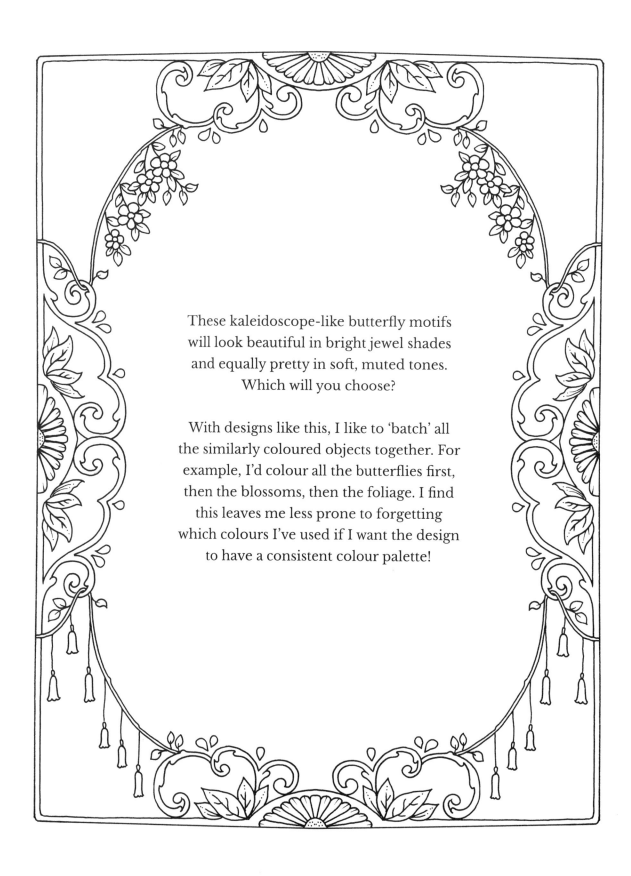

These kaleidoscope-like butterfly motifs
will look beautiful in bright jewel shades
and equally pretty in soft, muted tones.
Which will you choose?

With designs like this, I like to 'batch' all
the similarly coloured objects together. For
example, I'd colour all the butterflies first,
then the blossoms, then the foliage. I find
this leaves me less prone to forgetting
which colours I've used if I want the design
to have a consistent colour palette!

Adorned in patterns and embellishments, these pretty lanterns
are the perfect addition to any party.

Add details to the simple lanterns on the opposite page, using the ones
on this page as your inspiration. I'd suggest sketching in pencil first, then
going over your lines in pen. Once your strings of inky lanterns are
complete, consider adding some colour.

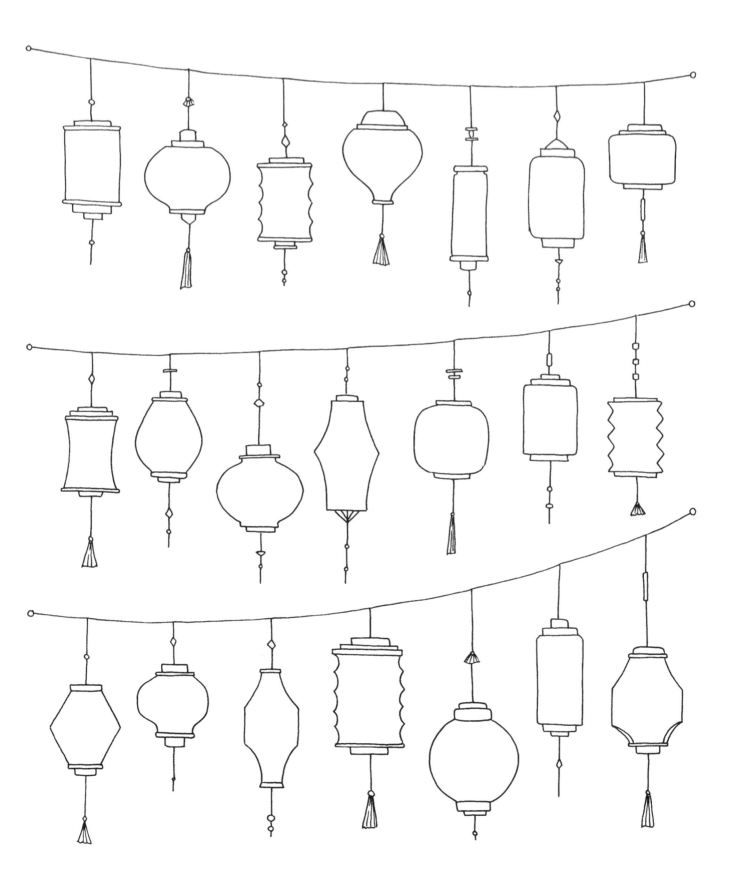

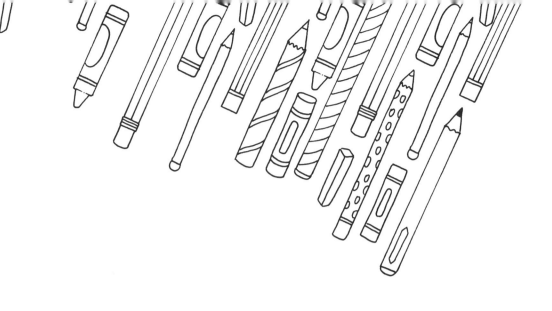

Hello, pencil lovers!

These are fun pages for colouring with all your favourite art supplies!
While the pattern is mainly pencils, there's also a few crayons
and pastels in there too.

Colour a few, colour them all – the choice is yours.
Just make sure to include all your favourite shades!

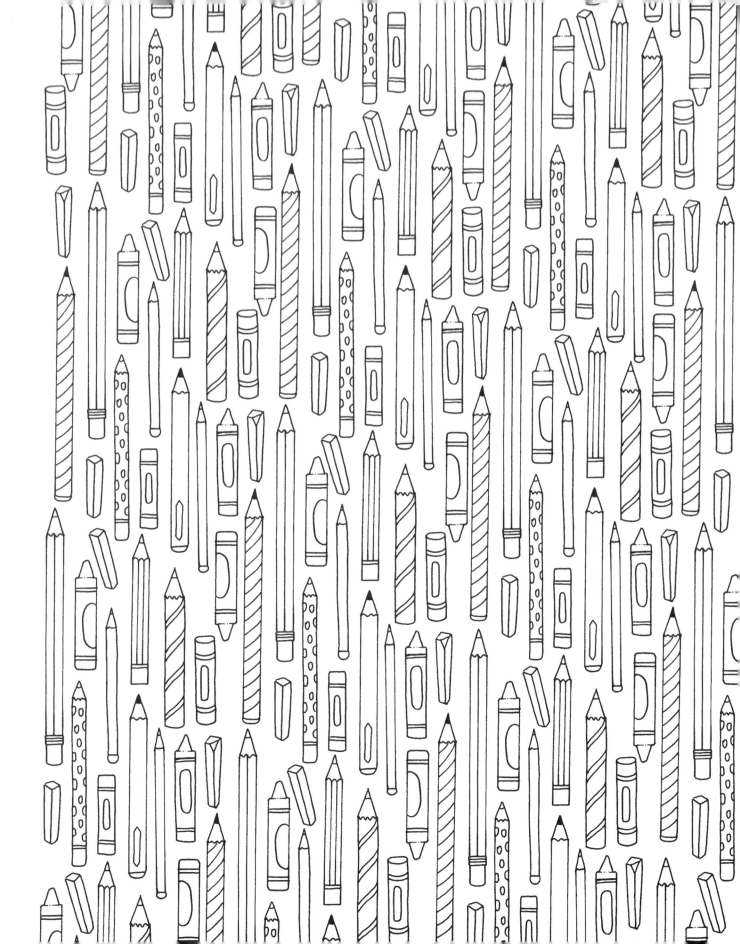

For me, flowers and nature are endlessly inspiring and constantly calming. There's no hustle and bustle here, just a couple of simple floral motifs waiting to flourish. Will you opt for delicate, muted tones or bold, tropical bright ones?

Fancy a little more flowers in your life?
Add some brilliant blooms to the leaves on this page!

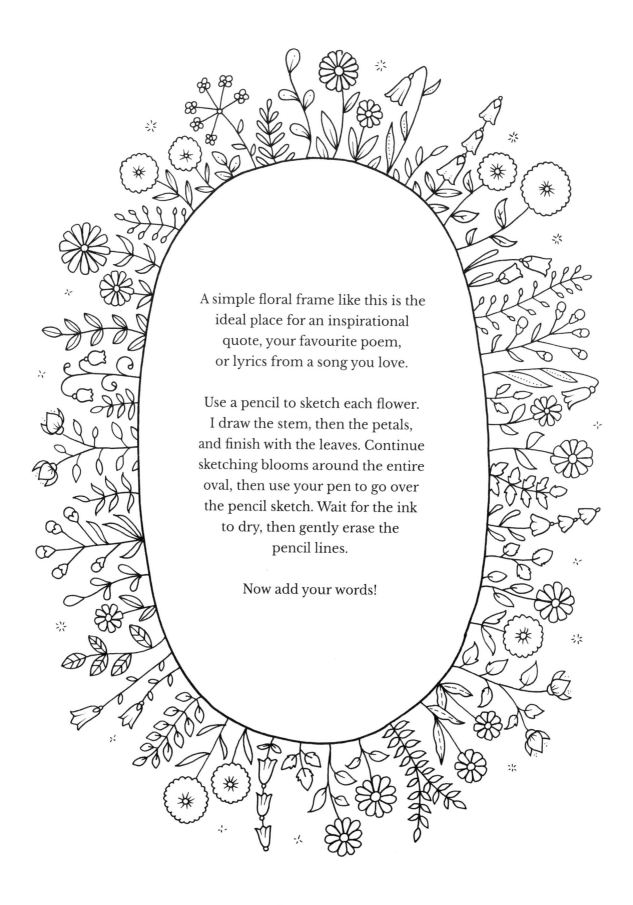

A simple floral frame like this is the
ideal place for an inspirational
quote, your favourite poem,
or lyrics from a song you love.

Use a pencil to sketch each flower.
I draw the stem, then the petals,
and finish with the leaves. Continue
sketching blooms around the entire
oval, then use your pen to go over
the pencil sketch. Wait for the ink
to dry, then gently erase the
pencil lines.

Now add your words!

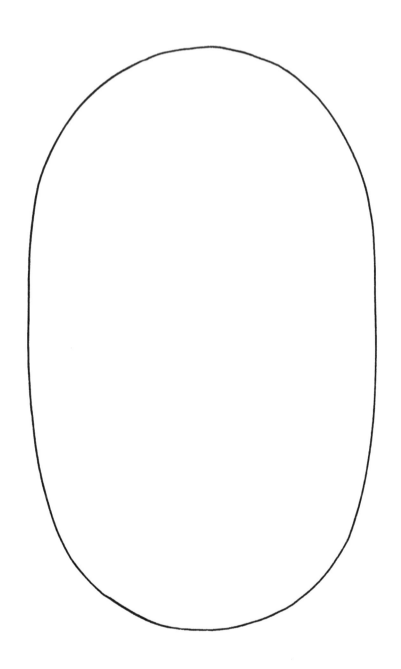

The End!

You did it! Congratulations on completing the 30 Days of Creativity challenge!
I hope you had fun and that this little book of nudges, prompts,
and ideas has kick-started your creativity!

But this isn't really the end.

It's actually just the beginning!

Now that you have started this creative journey, keep going!
Go back and complete some of the pages, add more details and embellishments
to others, and keep the momentum going!

You've got this!

Much love,

Johanna x.

Colour Palette Test Page

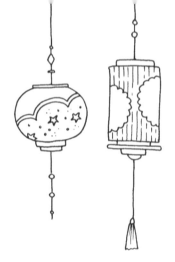

Colour Palette Test Page